Possessing The Promises of Rosh Hashanah

THE SUPERNATURAL SEASON FOR YOUR DIVINE TURNAROUND

~A Daily Devotional and Destiny Guide~

Dr. Michelle Corral

ISBN
ISBN-13: 978-1975748517

ISBN-10: 1975748514

TABLE OF CONTENTS

The Supernatural Season for Your Divine Turnaround

The Supernatural Season for Your Divine Turnaround

INTRODUCTION

Are you believing God for this Rosh Hashanah to be one of your life's most important dates with destiny? Rosh Hashanah is a time when God decrees our destinies for the next year. It is the time for that which He ordained for us before we were even born to reach its highest potential and purpose. This devotional is designed to enhance your firm determination for the highest elevation of destiny in your life.

There are three "destiny dynamics" in this devotional that I pray will lift the level of your destiny in the next year:

The first destiny dynamic is Acceleration:
I believe God wants to give you "precision vision" for this next year. The diligence of preparing a plan and setting goals fuels the fire of a destiny by design. Habakkuk 2:1-2 says, *"Write the vision, and make it plain upon the tables, that he may run that readeth it."*

The second destiny dynamic is Anticipation:

God has engineered every day in the month of Elul to be anticipated and designated by taking possession of the promises He performed on Rosh Hashanah. One of the definitions of the Hebrew word, *shana*, is "to repeat," which means what God did then, He will do again in your life.

The third destiny dynamic is Elevation:

I am believing God that you will reach the highest stratosphere of success that He has ordained for you this year. God wants you to walk in the "already" anointing.

In Deuteronomy 9:1, God told the children of Israel, *"Hear, O Israel: Thou art to pass over Jordan this day, to go in and possess nations greater and mightier than thyself, cities great and fenced up to heaven."* When God spoke that message through Moses to the nation of Israel, they did not pass over the Jordan until two months and ten days after the date it was spoken (Deuteronomy 1:1-3). Though the Lord specifically told them they were "to pass over

The Supernatural Season for Your Divine Turnaround

Jordan this day," that day did not actually happen until two months and ten days into the future.

God was speaking to a generation that was walking in an "already" anointing. The last line of Romans 4:17 says, *"and calleth those things which be not as though they were."* I truly believe this year is going to be one of acceleration, anticipation for the impossible, and highest elevation into the next dimension of destiny in your life!

To help keep you focused on achieving the possession of your promises, I highly encourage you to follow the "Disciplines of Destiny." I hope you will choose this book as the blueprint for your breakthrough, beloved. I am believing with you that there will be a performance of those things that the Lord has spoken to you, no matter how impossible they may seem. This is the season of the supernatural in your life!

Shana Tova,

Dr. Michelle Corral +

The Supernatural Season for Your Divine Turnaround

DAY 1

The Promise of Possession Over the Oppression of the Enemy

"And said, by myself have I sworn, saith the Lord, for because thou hast done this thing, and hast not withheld thy son, thine only son: That in blessing I will bless thee, and in multiplying I will multiply thy seed as the stars of the heaven, and as the sand which is upon the sea shore; and thy seed shall possess the gate of his enemies."
~Genesis 22:16-17~

God's promise for you to have breakthroughs in every battle is prophetically prefigured in one of the most miraculous moments with destiny ever recorded in the Bible. This powerful promise was bestowed on Rosh Hashanah at the time of the *Akedah Yitzhak* (the binding of Isaac). The Akedah Yitzhak is read all over the world on Rosh Hashanah because it was there on Mount Moriah

The Supernatural Season for Your Divine Turnaround

that God made His everlasting covenant with Abraham and his seed.

In a literal sense of Scripture, the binding of Isaac was Abrahams's 10th test that God ordained to be a *zechutz* (an inheritance by merit) for the seed of Abraham. Abraham's acquisition of the blessings and the inheritance obtained for his seed, by his obedience and willingness to sacrifice his only son unto God, all occurred on Rosh Hashanah.

The supernatural sign of God's faithfulness to perform His promise to the seed of Abraham, concerning possession of their enemy's gate, is symbolized in the *shofar* (ram's horn). The ram's horn of Rosh Hashanah prophetically parallels the substitutionary sacrifice God had provided for Abraham, instead of his son.

Genesis 22:13
And Abraham lifted up his eyes, and looked, and behold behind him a ram caught in a thicket by his horns: and Abraham went and took the ram, and offered him up for a burnt offering in the stead of his son.

Whenever God hears the sound of the shofar, He *remembers* the promise He had made to Abraham in the Akedah Yitzhak. The shofar symbolizes the substitutionary sacrifice of the ram, prefiguring the eternal sacrifice of Christ on the cross of Calvary. This means your Rosh Hashanah promise to possess the gate of your enemies is an inheritance (*zechutz*) that God has laid up for you through the cross of His only begotten Son.

This Rosh Hashanah, God is promising that you will overcome and triumph over every trial. God has given you exaltation over all your tribulation and every attack of the wicked one. The rabbinic saying of *Ma'aseh Avot Siman Lebanim*—meaning, "the actions of the *Avot* (fathers)"—as a sign for their children is understood in the Akedah Yitzhak. The actions of Abraham were a sign.

John 3:16
For God so loved the world, that he gave his only begotten Son that whosoever believeth in him should not perish, but have everlasting life.

The very victory God promised to Abraham's descendants in every battle, every trial, and every test has already been given to us as an inheritance in Christ.

Galatians 3:14
That the blessing of Abraham might come on the Gentiles through Jesus Christ; that we might receive the promise of the Spirit through faith.

Galatians 3:29
And if ye be Christ's, then are ye Abraham's seed, and heirs according to the promise.

Beloved, this means that the promise of possession over the oppression of the enemy, given on Rosh Hashanah to Abraham concerning his seed, is a Rosh Hashanah promise for you.

The Supernatural Season for Your Divine Turnaround

Prayer

Lord God, I give You praise that every enemy is under my feet. I want to give You glory that every principality and power coming against my family and my destiny is broken right now. I thank You for the Rosh Hashanah promise You have given me when You see the shofar and remember Your promise to Abraham and his descendants. I praise You that I will possess the gates of my enemies. By this, I know that You favor me, because my enemy will not triumph over me (Psalm 41:11), in the name of Jesus. Amen.

Spiritual Goals
Making Decisions for Destiny

1) Which areas of my life are oppressed by the enemy?

_____

_____

_____

_____

2) Do I know it is my Rosh Hashanah inheritance and promise to possess the gate of my enemies?

_____

_____

_____

_____

Blessing for Breakthrough Guide

Write a letter from your heart concerning the battles and the challenges you have had and how you are believing God to possess the gates of your enemies.

_____

_____

_____

_____

_____

_____

_____

_____

_____

_____

_____

_____

_____

_____

_____

_____

The Supernatural Season for Your Divine Turnaround

The Supernatural Season for Your Divine Turnaround

DAY 2

The Time of Restoration in Your Impossible Situation

"And when the seventh month was come, and the children of Israel were in their cities, the people gathered themselves together as one man to Jerusalem."
~**Ezra 3:1**~

In Ezra 3:1, the text teaches that it was in the seventh month after 70 years of Babylonian bondage that the courageous children of the captivity returned by faith from the land of darkness back into their destinies. Ezra goes out of his way to accentuate the seventh month as a significant sign of God's faithfulness to fulfill what He has promised.

In Ezra 3:6, the Bible documents the date of the seventh month as a significant sign of God's promise of providence during Rosh Hashanah: *"From the first day of the seventh month began they to offer burnt offerings unto the Lord. But the foundation of the temple of the Lord was not yet laid."* By emphasizing the seventh month in Ezra 3:1, the text is elaborating on how the Lord maneuvered the date to coincide with destiny. These dates give God glory by very apparently proving these things did not happen by coincidence. Instead, they were strategically planned by His power of providence.

All of the captives found themselves back in their place of promise, rebuilding the ruins of their desolated dreams. During this Rosh Hashanah, I believe God's promise to you is the same. These things were written in the word of God, not just so we know that they happened, but also so every generation who reads these things may know that what God did then, God will do again.

For the former captives, the most impossible dream was to be as "one man" in Jerusalem together in a place of desolated dreams. During this Rosh Hashanah, I believe God is going to bring you to the place of restoration in your impossible situation, just like He did for the children of Israel in Ezra 3:1-6. The broken down ruins of the temple are a prophetic parallel of the decimated dreams He will redeem this Rosh Hashanah.

The emphasis upon these dates is to demonstrate that man had absolutely nothing to do with these marvels. These are documented dates for the purpose of destiny so we may know that not all seasons are the same. Dates that coincide with destiny help us understand the difference between a secular segment of time and the "set" time God has ordained to be propitious for His predestined plan in your life. During this Rosh Hashanah, He is going to put you back into your place of promise.

In Ezra 3:6, the Bible tells us, *"from the first day of the seventh month they began to offer burnt offerings unto the Lord."* In Ezra 3:3, the text teaches how the children of Israel had set up *"the altar on his bases."* In a personal prophetic sense of Scripture, Ezra was showing us the very first thing that was done on the first day of the new year was to re-establish the sacrificial system. The darkness of exile was based upon the fact that there was no temple in Babylon and, therefore, no sacrifice. The temple uniquely and prophetically prefigures our service of sacrifice unto God.

The Babylonian captivity is a type of bondage and spiritual captivity that prophetically parallels a life without sacrificial service to God. Once the "altar" is rebuilt in your life, beloved, the proper foundation for your new year will be laid.

Prayer

Dear Jesus, I believe You are placing me back into the place of promise, no matter how difficult the dilemma. I believe, even now You are preparing Your people and Your plan for my miracle on Rosh Hashanah. I claim that I will take back the territory, rebuild the altar, and begin offering sacrifices unto You at the beginning of this new year. Lord, I believe that as I set the altar of sacrifice as the priority in my life, the "Temple" (Your presence on earth and my destiny) shall be rebuilt. Amen.

Spiritual Goals
Making Decisions for Destiny

1) Do I set goals to establish daily sacrifice in my life because I love God above all things?

_____

_____

_____

_____

2) Which areas of my life were in a state of compromise in the last year?

_____

_____

_____

_____

3) Have I noticed the diminishing of my dreams and goals for the Kingdom as a result of my double-mindedness?

_____

_____

_____

_____

Blessing for Breakthrough Guide

Daily ask the Holy Spirit for the grace to be consciously aware of secret fears and spiritual anxieties that may cause you to remain in a place of delayed destiny.

_____

_____

_____

_____

_____

_____

_____

_____

_____

_____

_____

_____

_____

The Supernatural Season for Your Divine Turnaround

_____

_____

_____

_____

_____

_____

_____

_____

_____

_____

_____

_____

_____

_____

_____

_____

_____

_____

_____

_____

_____

_____

_____

_____

DAY 3

Promise of the Miraculous Memorial

"Speak unto the children of Israel, saying, In the seventh month, in the first day of the month, shall ye have a sabbath, a memorial of blowing of trumpets, an holy convocation."
~Leviticus 23:24~

"... and Elkanah knew Hannah his wife; and the Lord remembered her."
~1 Samuel 1:19b~

Leviticus 23:24 teaches that one of the most essential elements of Rosh Hashanah is that this feast of celebration for the new year is also known as "a day of remembrance." In Hebrew, it is referred to as the *Yom HaZikaron*. It was on this feast of Rosh Hashanah that God remembered His beloved daughter, Hannah, just as He will remember you.

We are introduced to Hannah in the book of 1 Samuel, Chapter 1. In 1 Samuel 1:3, the text teaches us the price Hannah paid to annually go up to the house of the Lord *"to worship and to sacrifice unto the Lord of hosts in Shiloh."* In a literal sense of Scripture, the text is referring to the yearly pilgrimage festivals that were required of the Israelites, three times a year for each of the three major Biblical feasts. Before Jerusalem was established as the holy city, Shiloh was originally instituted by Joshua to be the holy place of God's presence during the pilgrimage feasts.

Though 1 Samuel 1 does not specify which of the major three pilgrimage feasts occurred in the narrative, by using the phrase *"and the Lord remembered,"* the text indicates that the pilgrimage going up to Shiloh was during Rosh Hashanah. It was not required for women to go up during the feast. However, Scripture teaches us that these feasts were still a major priority to Hannah. Her faithfulness to God teaches us one of the most profound principles of accessing the impossible in our lives. We learn from the text that as Hannah went up every year to Shiloh, her adversary (Peninnah) provoked her.

1 Samuel 1:6-7
"And her adversary also provoked her sore, for to make her fret, because the Lord had shut up her womb. And as He did so year by year, when she went up to the house of the Lord, so she provoked her; therefore she wept, and did not eat."

Beloved, this means that Hannah's strong belief in God's powerful presence during the time of the Biblical feasts was what caused her to be so determined for her destiny. Hannah's example teaches us how to never settle for anything but God's best in our lives, no matter how difficult the dilemma may seem. In order to get to Shiloh, she had to press past her adversary, who constantly became a source of discouragement, trial, and testing for her.

Hannah leaves an example for us: though she was taunted with degradation, it produced the determination she needed to not be denied her destiny.

The Supernatural Season for Your Divine Turnaround

<u>1 Samuel 1:11</u>

"And she vowed a vow, and said, O Lord of hosts, if Thou wilt indeed look on the affliction of Thine handmaid, and remember me, and not forget Thine handmaid, but wilt give unto Thine handmaid a man child, then I will give him unto the Lord all the days of his life, and there shall no razor come upon his head."

When Hannah arrived in Shiloh, her desperation brought forth a consecration unto God. In her prayer, she revealed the secret of Rosh Hashanah. The text takes us to its emphasis by the phrases *"remember"* and *"not forget."* In a Hebraic sense of Scripture, the author was emphasizing the Day of Remembrance, which is Rosh Hashanah. She promised that if the Lord gave her a son, she would lend *"him unto the Lord all the days of his life."* Hannah's prayer teaches us how she believed by faith that Rosh Hashanah would be a day of remembrance for her.

On Rosh Hashanah, the promise of a miraculous memorial became the source of breakthrough for Hannah. The text teaches in 1 Samuel 1:19, *"And they rose up in the morning early, and worshipped before the Lord, and returned, and came to their house to Ramah: and Elkanah knew Hannah his wife; and the Lord remembered her."* Beloved, this means Hannah conceived Samuel the prophet on Rosh Hashanah. Many of us who can identify with the feelings she had felt—wondering if we are forgotten, or thinking we are the last one in line to receive our blessing—can also press our way into our promise, just as Hannah did.

God promises that as you prepare for this holy season, He will not forget you. Just continue in the anointing to press your way into the promises. Hebrews 6:10 says: *"For God is not unrighteous to forget your work and labor of love, which you have showed toward His Name, in that ye have ministered to the saints, and do minister."*

I hear God saying: "You have been faithful and courageous in the midst of great opposition. Continue to trust Me. Have I ever failed you, My child?"

The Supernatural Season for Your Divine Turnaround

Prayer

Lord Jesus, I ask You to prepare me for Rosh Hashanah. Only You know the secrets of my heart. Give me the grace to keep trusting You, and the fortitude to keep pressing passed all of the obstacles that would keep me stuck in a state of disappointment. I want to believe You for the impossible. If I need to make a consecration of fasting and prayer, I ask You to reveal it to my soul. I want this petition not for myself, but for the Kingdom. Give me the grace of right "intentions" (kavanot). Search me, oh God, and know my heart. Let this petition be used for Your glory. I claim it, I believe it, and I will not doubt, in the name of Jesus. Amen!

Spiritual Goals
Making Decisions for Destiny

1) Have I been "passionate" or "passive" toward what God has called me to do?

_____
_____
_____
_____

2) Have I allowed a circumstance similar to the one Hannah had with Peninnah to discourage me from going forward into my destiny?

_____
_____
_____
_____

3) Has the ungodly resistance produced in me a greater persistence in prayer towards my dream?

_____
_____
_____
_____

Breakthrough for Blessing Guide

Study and confess Scripture verses on God's faithfulness in rewarding diligence.

_____

_____

_____

_____

_____

_____

_____

_____

_____

_____

_____

_____

_____

_____

_____

_____

_____

_____

The Supernatural Season for Your Divine Turnaround

DAY 4

The Mordecai Miracle

"On that night could not the king sleep, and he commanded to bring the book of records of the chronicles; and they were read before the king."
~Esther 6:1~

Rosh Hashanah is the day when "the books" are opened in heaven. Scripture teaches us in Revelation 20:12, *"And I saw the dead, small and great, stand before God; and the books were opened: and another book was opened, which is the book of life: and the dead were judged out of those things which were written in the books, according to their works."*

The Bible also teaches us in Malachi 3:16 that *"they that feared the Lord spake often one to another: and the Lord hearkened, and heard it, and a book of remembrance was written before Him for them that feared the Lord, and that thought upon his Name."*

The Supernatural Season for Your Divine Turnaround

Have you ever been in a predicament where someone took the credit for something you did? And to make matters even worse, did this predicament come with such an undermining of your good name that it terribly destroyed your reputation on top of it all? If we multiply a situation such as this to the tenth degree, we can only imagine what God's righteous servant, Mordecai, experienced.

In Esther 2, the text teaches: *"In those days, while Mordecai sat in the king's gate, two of the king's chamberlains, Bigthan and Teresh, of those which kept the door, were wroth and sought to lay hands on the king Ahasuerus. And the thing was known to Mordecai, who told it unto Esther the queen; and Esther certified the king thereof in Mordecai's name"* (Esther 2:21-22).

After the text tells us of this incredible act of loyalty on behalf of Mordecai, Scripture immediately indicates the following in Esther 3:1, *"After these things did king Ahasuerus promote Haman the son of Hammedatha the Agagite, and advanced him, and set his seat above all the princes that were with him."* This means that Haman not only took all the credit that rightfully belonged to

Mordecai, he even began a series of devious plots to undermine this righteous man.

On the day that Haman sought to plan Mordecai's execution, divine providence through the hidden hand of heaven maneuvered a miracle for Mordecai. The text wants us to be completely aware that this deliverance occurred as a Rosh Hashanah miracle. Scripture does not want us to consider this supernatural setup to have merely been a coincidence, for it was definitely the power of providence working on behalf of Mordecai.

Esther 6:1
On that night could not the king sleep, and he commanded to bring the book of records of the chronicles; and they were read before the king.

The reading of Esther 6:1 in the Hebrew language is slightly different from the English version. In Hebrew, it translates as "he commanded to bring the book of *remembrance*" (not the book of records). This verse also indicates that it was King Ahasuerus who opened the book of remembrance, but the text was actually referring to the King of Heaven. Beloved, whenever Scripture wants to show us the King of Heaven moving on behalf of

His people in the book of Esther, it eliminates the name *Ahasuerus*.

Rosh Hashanah, also known as the Day of Remembrance, was the very day God brought forth a divine reversal for Mordecai and gave him the honor that Haman sought for himself. When the king asked Haman what should be done unto a man whom the king would delight to honor, the text teaches: *"Now Haman thought in his heart, To whom would the King delight to do honour more than to myself?"* (Esther 6:6).

The text is also showing us how, on the day of Rosh Hashanah, the reward that should have gone to Mordecai earlier was now being increased beyond what he could even ask or think! Furthermore, it happened to be his greatest enemy, Haman, who ordered the increase of this reward, thinking that it would be given to him. I believe Rosh Hashanah is the day of release for all of the rewards that have been held up for many of you. It is because Rosh Hashanah is the day our destinies are set for the next year.

Many of God's precious people have labored and have not fainted. You may have wondered why it has been so difficult. You may be asking God, "I see everyone else being blessed, but when is my turn coming, dear Lord?" During this season, I believe that God is going to release great rewards to you, beyond what you can even ask or imagine, just as he did for Mordecai. Our God sees your faithfulness, and He is the Rewarder of those who diligently seek Him (Hebrews 11:6), for, behold, His reward is with Him, and His work before Him (Isaiah 40:10b).

As we prepare for Rosh Hashanah, let us continue to have pure hearts of forgiveness toward those who have injured us. Let us not hold a grudge, or use revenge in the form of critical thinking or evil speaking toward anyone who may have used us, or abused our friendship and our love for them.

Matthew 5:44
But I say unto you, Love your enemies, bless them that curse you, do good to them that hate you, and pray for them which despitefully use you, and persecute you.

Beloved, if our hearts are pure and do not condemn us (1 John 3:21), then we will have confidence toward God, knowing that whatever we ask of Him according to His will, He will hear us (1 John 5:14). He will prepare a table before you in the presence of your enemies (Psalm 23:5) as you walk in such purity of heart without guile.

The Supernatural Season for Your Divine Turnaround

Prayer

Wonderful Jesus, today I ask You to prepare my heart for Rosh Hashanah. I ask You to give me the grace to forgive my enemies. Guide my speech and my thoughts by Your grace to neither be critical nor take any type of revenge against those who injured me. I trust completely in Your Word, for You are the Rewarder of those who diligently seek You. Please open my eyes so that I will not miss even one of the blessings that I know You will bestow upon me this season. Help me to receive the gift of thankfulness and gratefulness for everything You do for me, in the name of Jesus. Amen.

Spiritual Goals
Making Decisions for Destiny

1) Is there someone I have not forgiven because they injured me or took away something that belonged to me?

_____
_____
_____
_____

2) When I think of those who have hurt me in any way, is there a tinge of critical thinking toward them? Am I asking God for the grace to walk as Jesus walked toward others, as well as the grace to pray for them?

_____
_____
_____
_____

3) Can I see the great good God has brought out of this situation, similar to the "Mordecai miracle"?

_____
_____
_____
_____

Breakthrough for Blessing Guide

Study the Scriptures and confess how God has promised that your enemies will not triumph over you.

See Psalm 25:2 and Psalm 41:11, and apply these verses to your life.

_____

_____

_____

_____

_____

_____

_____

_____

_____

_____

_____

_____

_____

_____

The Supernatural Season for Your Divine Turnaround

_____

_____

_____

_____

_____

_____

_____

_____

_____

_____

_____

_____

_____

_____

_____

_____

_____

_____

_____

_____

DAY 5

The Miracle of Clarity Out of Your Confusion

"In the beginning God created the heaven and the earth. And the earth was without form, and void; and darkness was upon the face of the deep. And the Spirit of God moved upon the face of the waters."
~Genesis 1:1-2~

The supernatural significance of Rosh Hashanah is hidden in the first two verses of the book of Genesis. Rosh Hashanah is the anniversary of the creation of the universe. The rabbinic sages determined the date of this event by transposing the Hebrew letters of the very first word in the Bible: *bereshit. Bereshit* literally means "in the beginning" in Hebrew. By delving into the depths of each letter in the Torah, these dedicated men of God discovered that, upon rearranging the letters in the word *bereshit* ("in the beginning"), the phrase *aleph b'Tishri* became apparent. Translated from Hebrew to English, *aleph b'Tishri* literally means "on the first of Tishri"—the first day of the seventh month on the Hebrew calendar—which is Rosh Hashanah.

When applying an exegesis on the next verse, we see what occurred on the very first Rosh Hashanah recorded in Scripture: *"And the earth was without form, and void; and darkness was upon the face of the deep. And the Spirit of God moved upon the face of the waters"* (Genesis 1:2). Literally, "without form" in Hebrew is the phrase: *haytah tohu va-bohu.* The two Hebrew words, *tohu va-bohu*, help us understand what God did on the very first Rosh Hashanah. The word *tohu* means "waste, desolation, or wilderness." The word *bohu* is a word that is used to describe indistinguishable ruin and vacuity.

The text also teaches that "*darkness was upon the face of the deep.*" The Hebrew word used to describe this darkness is the word, *choshek.* This word does not just indicate the absence of light, but describes a sense of chaos, confusion, and commotion that was over the face of the waters. Here, the text is teaching us that God's Spirit is bringing His order (*seder*) into all chaos and confusion, re-emphasizing the re-creation over devastation.

In a personal prophetic sense of Scripture, the Biblical feasts are seasons set in the heavens. God's revelation of these feasts were inscribed in the first seven days of Creation. Since these feasts govern time, the highest purpose of time is in the significance of these Biblical feasts and the seasons in which they are celebrated.

Genesis 1:14

And God said, Let there be lights in the firmament of the heaven to divide the day from the night; and let them be for signs, and for seasons, and for days, and years.

Genesis 1:14 illustrates the fourth day of creation for us. Scripture goes out of its way to enunciate the highest purpose of time by using the hermeneutical principle of interpretation that considers the item mentioned first in the verse to be most important. Genesis 1:14 articulates the meaning of "*and let them be for signs and for seasons, and for days, and years.*" In a personal prophetic sense of Scripture, you may prophetically parallel your destiny with that which is "without form and void," especially if it is in a place of confusion or indistinguishable ruin. But I believe God is saying this to you today: "I am going to take all of the chaos and confusion over your destiny and bring divine order into it. I have a purpose out of this pain."

You may not know it now, but God's predestined plan over your destiny means He can take that which is without form and void and bring forth great purpose and plans for His honor and glory. You may be blaming yourself for mistakes you made in the past. But I believe God is saying to you today: "I am the One who turns mistakes into miracles."

Perhaps you have suffered great loss and devastation. You may be grieving over what once was. You may feel in your heart that it could never be like it was before. But God has given us the gift of these Biblical feasts—supernatural segments of time when divine providence brings destiny out of our darkness.

Going back to Scripture and following the text systematically, we see that Genesis 1:3-4 says:

The Supernatural Season for Your Divine Turnaround

"And God said, Let there be light: and there was light. And God saw the light, and that it was good: and God divided the light from the darkness." This means that when God brought divine order over the chaos on the first day of creation, He also brought light out of the darkness. Beloved one, He is doing the same thing right now in your life.

The Hebrew word for "light" is the word *ohr*, which also has a parallel meaning for "victory, salvation, strength." Psalm 27:1 says, *"The Lord is my light and my salvation; whom shall I fear? the Lord is the strength of my life; of whom shall I be afraid?"* God is bringing light out of the darkest days of your life. He is bringing forth salvation, strength, healing, deliverance, joy, revelation, illumination, victory, clarity, and unlimited blessings and miracles in the midst of the darkness. This Rosh Hashanah, let us continue to believe and trust that God will bring a great plan out of what was so painful in your life!

The Supernatural Season for Your Divine Turnaround

Prayer

Dear Lord Jesus, I ask You this very moment to take the chaos, the confusion, the darkness, the unknown, my mistakes, etc. and turn them into miracles. I ask that Your Holy Spirit would move over the face of my destiny, which may currently seem without form and void. Let the anointing begin to transform my destiny into Your highest pinnacle of purpose for me this Rosh Hashanah and throughout the year. I trust You to do this, my Lord, and I know it begins with loving You above all things. When I love You above all things—for nothing can ever be compared to You and my love for You—then everything shall be in divine order, in the name of Jesus. Amen.

The Supernatural Season for Your Divine Turnaround

Spiritual Goals
Making Decisions for Destiny

1) Do I feel like my life is in confusion and out of order? Is it out of order because my spiritual life has been out of order? How do I resolve to place my life back in order?

_____

_____

_____

_____

2) Have I placed my love for God above all other loves in my life? Have I placed the things of the Kingdom as secondary to secular things?

_____

_____

_____

_____

3) Which areas in my life lack order, discipline, and consistency?

_____

_____

_____

_____

The Supernatural Season for Your Divine Turnaround

4) Am I focused on what His perfect will is, and am I working daily to accomplish it?

_____

_____

_____

_____

Breakthrough for Blessing Guide

Ask the Lord for a healthy balance between putting His Kingdom first and loving Him above all things, while also experiencing the special time He is giving you for your soul to be filled and refreshed by His Spirit.

Ask the Holy Spirit for your Destiny Plan for the upcoming year.

_____

_____

_____

_____

_____

_____

_____

_____

_____

_____

_____

_____

The Supernatural Season for Your Divine Turnaround

DAY 6

Experiencing God's Best After the Test

"So all the elders of Israel came to the king to Hebron; and king David made a league with them in Hebron before the Lord: and they anointed David king over Israel.... In Hebron he reigned over Judah seven years and six months: and in Jerusalem he reigned thirty and three years over all Israel and Judah."
~2 Samuel 5: 3, 5~

Have you ever wondered, "God, how long?" Our heartfelt feelings and questions after years of tears are expressed in the phrase: *How long?* For King David, waiting on God's word for the performance of promises took many years. In 1 Samuel 16:13, David was anointed by the prophet Samuel to be king over Israel. The text teaches that, though he had a powerful prophecy over his life, the full manifestation of exultation into his destiny did not happen until many years later.

David was presented with a series of tests. The most difficult dilemma was his very personal and private pain concerning his own father-in-law, King Saul. Throughout the book of 1 Samuel, the text teaches us about the saga of sufferings David endured in the form of lies, accusations, jealousies, injustices, faults, and endless traps to snare his soul.

David was a more-than-qualified warrior who, in self-defense, could have easily defeated King Saul. However, Scripture documents details of his inward spiritual battle, in addition to the exterior one. The composition of the text contrasts these two types of character tests. David was able to perceive this test. He did not consider the pressure and circumstances to be his greatest challenge. Instead, he earnestly sought the Lord's help to put a guard on his mouth not to sin, neither by speaking evil against Saul nor by taking any form of revenge against him.

The Supernatural Season for Your Divine Turnaround

Psalm 39:1-2

I said, I will take heed to my ways, that I sin not with my tongue: I will keep my mouth with a bridle, while the wicked is before me. I was dumb with silence, I held my peace, even from good; and my sorrow was stirred.

In Psalm 37, the context conveys that David's primary concern was not the unbearable pain and difficulty of this excruciating test. On the contrary, David's prayer to God was that he would be protected from retaliating, speaking evil, or becoming angry at his adversary. This was a very unusual test for David since the Scripture describes him in 1 Samuel 16 as being *ruddy*. This term not only means "handsome," it can also mean "red" in an idiomatic sense to illustrate how easily angered he was.

The most important component of this crisis was to stay in the secret place of the Most High. This meant that David knew this test was not about apparent trials or exterior tribulations. It was specifically about staying pure in his heart before God. David perceived that Saul's relentless search to pursue him daily in the wilderness of Judea was likened unto a lion hunting his soul. This means David knew the true test was in his interior being.

The soul is the seat of the emotions. The lion pursuing his soul represents those adverse circumstances designed to rile up his emotions toward anger and revenge. In Psalm 18:20, the text teaches that David alluded to the day of his coronation as the passing of all examinations for his destiny.

Psalm 7:2
Lest he tear my soul like a lion, rending it in pieces, while there is none to deliver.

Psalm 18:20
The Lord rewarded me according to my righteousness; according to the cleanness of my hands hath he recompensed me.

Psalm 18:23
I was also upright before Him, and I kept myself from mine iniquity.

In 2 Samuel 5:5, Scripture goes out of its way to tell us that the final fulfillment of God's promises was bestowed upon David during Rosh Hashanah.

The Supernatural Season for Your Divine Turnaround

It reads: "*In Hebron he reigned over Judah seven years and six months*" ("six months" signifies the time period until the 29th of Elul). Then, the text proceeds to tell us that "*in Jerusalem he reigned thirty and three years over all Israel and Judah.*" This means that he began his reign as king over all Israel and Judah on Rosh Hashanah, which is the first day of the seventh month. The 29th of Elul is the end of this six-month period. I believe God is saying to you, "Beloved, as you keep your heart pure from guile, so will I do for you as I did for David. Fear not, for I will be still upon you and grant you My best after this test."

This Rosh Hashanah, as we examine our hearts to be free from any form of revenge—such as speaking against someone who hurt us—God will open doors of destiny for you like he did for David. I believe this is your season. You have not come this far to be denied destiny now. Let it be your quest to remove all malice and anger, even if it is justifiable, and just walk in love. As you walk in love, you will abide in Him.

The Supernatural Season for Your Divine Turnaround

John 15:7

If you abide in Me and My words abide in you, you shall ask what you will and it shall be done unto you.

Prayer

Dear Jesus, I ask You, Son of David, to have mercy upon me. I want to follow in Your footsteps and do what You have asked me to do. I want to truly love my enemies, and pray for those who persecute me and despitefully use me. Please help me not to think any evil against them or repay evil for evil, but instead render good unto those who have done me harm. I ask You to prepare me for the mighty promises of Rosh Hashanah. I claim that You will do for me what You did for King David. I fully accept and fully receive, as well as look forward to and anticipate Your best after this test, in the name of Jesus. Amen.

Spiritual Goals
Making Decisions for Destiny

1) Is there anger or resentment (a form of anger that lies within the heart) in my heart toward someone who did harm against me or my reputation?

_____

_____

_____

_____

2) Do I think any less of a person who spoke against me? Can I see that person as Christ sees them? Am I willing to ask God to help me in this?

_____

_____

_____

_____

3) Am I willing to pay any price for the destiny that Jesus suffered and died for to give me?

_____

_____

_____

_____

Breakthrough for Blessing Guide

Keep a journal that will help you monitor motives in your conscience.

Spend time every day in prayer alone with God for at least 15 to 20 minutes.

Write down the promises that He has given you, whether from His word or in prayer for this year.

Anticipate and expect the fullest potential of His promises to you, and do not settle for anything less than His best for you!

_____

_____

_____

_____

_____

_____

_____

_____

_____

_____

_____

The Supernatural Season for Your Divine Turnaround

DAY 7

The Finishing Factor

Being confident of this very thing, that he which hath begun a good work in you will perform it until the day of Jesus Christ.
~Philippians 1:6~

Is there a special assignment during the past year that you failed to finish? There can be many excuses we have accumulated, whether sincerely legitimate or not, that will answer why we failed to finish. One of the most prevalent reasons why we detour off the path to destiny is distraction. Distractions can become disastrous to a destiny. God has promised us in His word that we can overcome this detriment to our destinies. God has promised us that, no matter how fierce the fight, we will finish.

God has given us His guarantee that one of the works of grace is the "finishing factor," as we see in Hebrews 12:2a, which says, "*Looking unto Jesus the author and finisher of our faith.*" Beloved, this promise means that the finishing factor through the grace of God has enabled us to overcome every obstacle that would pull us off the path of purpose and promise.

One of the greatest Biblical examples of overcoming obstacles that prevent us from completing God's divine design of destiny for our lives is Nehemiah. Nehemiah was chosen by God for the insurmountable task of rebuilding the ruins of Zion. His unique assignment was to rebuild the ruins of the walls. The text teaches us this task was accomplished in 52 days: "*So the wall was finished in the twenty and fifth day of the month of Elul, in fifty and two days*" (Nehemiah 6:15).

The book of Nehemiah shows us that, in order to focus until we are finished, there are "Disciplines for Destiny."

The 1st Discipline for Destiny is the Completion Concept:

In Nehemiah 6:3, the text teaches that there were persons sent by their enemies to distract them off the project: "*And I sent messengers unto them, saying, I am doing a great work, so that I cannot come down: why should the work cease, whilst I leave it, and come down to you?"* Nehemiah refused to cease in his service to God for anything. He considered ceasing this important work on the project as coming down. He used the phrase "come down" twice in the verse because he recognized the distraction against his destiny.

The 2nd Discipline for Destiny is to Finish in Phases and Set a Deadline:

Finishing in phases can give us motivation against intimidation, regarding the immensity of a project. The context conveys how the 52 days demonstrated that Nehemiah was working with deadlines. This means he had set goals to be accomplished in each phase in order to finish the entire project in a timely manner.

The 3rd Discipline for Destiny is the Power of Prayer Over the Project:

Nehemiah 4:8-9 says, "*And conspired all of them together to come and fight against Jerusalem, and to hinder it. Nevertheless we made our prayer unto our God, and set a watch against them day and night, because of them.*" Beloved, I believe God is calling you into the highest pinnacle of purpose this Rosh Hashanah. He will give you the strength and the discipline to fulfill all assignments of the past year so He can lavish upon you the highest design of destiny in the coming year. It is His will for you to complete what He called you to do.

Luke 14:28

For which of you, intending to build a tower, sitteth not down first, and counteth the cost, whether he have sufficient to finish it?

Beloved, let us put our future in fast forward by leaving nothing undone.

The Supernatural Season for Your Divine Turnaround

Prayer

Lord Jesus, I claim the anointing and the victory of the finishing factor over all You have given me in the past year. Holy Spirit, give me the fortitude to face all uncompleted projects. I claim the anointing to finish every assignment and take each of them to another level of perfection. Give me the grace of perseverance in every project, and let me not fall out before the completion. Let my trademark be one of excellence for Your glory. Help me fulfill all my commitments and grant me the disciplines for destiny, in the name of Jesus. Amen.

Spiritual Goals
Making Decisions for Destiny

1) Have I fulfilled my commitments in every area of my life?

_____

_____

_____

_____

2) Is there a project God gave me that I failed to finish?

_____

_____

_____

_____

3) Are there inconsistencies in my character that contradict integrity and discipline?

_____

_____

_____

_____

The Supernatural Season for Your Divine Turnaround

4) Where can I begin *tikkun middot* (character correction) in my life?

_____

_____

_____

_____

Breakthrough for Blessing Guide

Finish all incomplete projects by the 29th of Elul (the day before Rosh Hashanah).

Complete any unfulfilled prayer assignments.

Prepare a plan for the new year!

_____

_____

_____

_____

_____

_____

_____

_____

_____

_____

_____

_____

_____

DAY 8

Your Highest Pinnacle of Purpose in the New Year: Lech Lecha
"Go to Yourself, Go for Yourself"

"Now the Lord had said unto Abram, Get thee out of thy country, and from thy kindred, and from thy father's house, unto a land that I will shew thee."
~Genesis 12:1~

Have you ever asked the question: "What is the highest pinnacle of purpose in my life?" When God called Abram to be the father of the Jewish people and be the founder of the nation of Israel, He said to him, "*Lech lecha.*" In the Hebrew language, *lech lecha* means "go to yourself." It can also mean "go *for* yourself." God's incredible call to Abram required that he encounter his true self by following His perfect will. God's definition of *destiny* included the essential requirement of severing soul ties from the past in order to go forward into the future.

This Rosh Hashanah, God is calling you to walk toward the highest dimension of your destiny. As Abraham was called, so are we also called. Genesis 12:1 teaches us the supernatural success secret of Lech Lecha in our own lives. These things were written so that we might apply these principles when paving the pathway for our destinies.

The depths of destiny revealed in Lech Lecha must be understood in context. In Genesis 11:31, the text teaches that *"Terah took Abram his son, and Lot the son of Haran his son's son, and Sarai his daughter in law, his son Abram's wife; and they went forth with them from Ur of the Chaldees, to go into the land of Canaan; and they came unto Haran, and dwelt there."* One of the most obvious obstacles to the concept of Lech Lecha can be seen in the context of this verse. Terah had set out for Canaan, but only went halfway on his journey. The context conveys that *"they went forth with them from Ur of the Chaldees, to go into the land of Canaan,"* but then dwelt in Haran, which was halfway to their original destination. The text indicates that Terah had fallen out before finishing what he had set forth to do.

This new year, let us ask the Lord for the grace to fulfill and finish every task He has given us to do. This evident character trait is the context by which the Lord called Abram. Abram would not fall out, but would finish every assignment God had given him to fulfill, which is a key component to Lech Lecha. In this difficult call of Lech Lecha (going to yourself), there will be many excruciating emotional, spiritual, and physical challenges.

The first spiritual stepping stone is being willing to pay any price to do God's will. Abram had to leave every kind of ungodly, man-made, false security system in order to experience Lech Lecha. God tested Abram to go forward in faith, even without him fully knowing where he was going. In Genesis 12:7, the text teaches that *"the Lord appeared unto Abram, and said, Unto thy seed will I give this land."* It was only when he had obeyed God by taking a step of blind faith going forward that the next spiritual segment of the vision was revealed to him. From this, we learn how "activation produces revelation." This means that,

The Supernatural Season for Your Divine Turnaround

as Abram went forward in obedience to God's will (activation), God released the next level of his call (revelation). This new year, as God calls you forth into the highest pinnacle of your purpose, it will require faithful determination and relentless perseverance for you to experience the highest elevation of God's will for your life.

In Genesis 12:10, the text teaches that, as soon as Abram came into Canaan, there was a grievous famine in the land. At this point, Abram had two choices: 1) retreat and return to Haran, his kin, his country, and his father's house, or 2) go into Egypt. Choosing Egypt would mean placing his life in severe danger, since Egyptian law had required Pharaoh's servants to kidnap all the beautiful women they could find in the land, and then kill their husbands. Pressed with such a difficult decision—between one that seemed like an easy fix (but would tragically forfeit his destiny), and another that would completely endanger his life—Abram had chosen the one that required his total trust in God.

This Rosh Hashanah, may you go to your true and completed self, beloved. This call of Lech Lecha means that you shall go forward in faith. This year, we shall not fall out before we finish. We will sever all ungodly soul ties, and never turn back!

Prayer

Dearest Holy Spirit, I ask You to enable me to go forward and to not fall out, no matter how challenging the task. I ask You to enable me to go forward by faith. I ask for all ungodly soul ties from every relationship that will keep me stuck in the past to be broken now. Release me into the new anointing for the fresh new appointing. I ask You for the grace to never turn back. Lord, bring me into my true identity and my true self, which can only be known by Your perfect will in my life, in the name of Jesus. Amen.

Spiritual Goals
Making Decisions for Destiny

1) Is there something holding back "Lech Lecha" in my life?

_____

_____

_____

_____

2) Have I turned back because of pressure in the past year? How will I resolve it?

_____

_____

_____

_____

3) Are there soul ties in my heart and/or emotions that are pulling me back into the past and need to be severed?

_____

_____

_____

_____

Breakthrough for Blessing Guide

If there are any areas you committed yourself to in the last year and failed to finish, may you complete the task before the new year. Reprogram your life away from any ungodly dependencies or soul ties that will paralyze and immobilize your destiny.

_____

_____

_____

_____

_____

_____

_____

_____

_____

_____

_____

_____

_____

_____

The Supernatural Season for Your Divine Turnaround

_____

_____

_____

_____

_____

_____

_____

_____

_____

_____

_____

_____

_____

_____

_____

_____

_____

_____

_____

_____

_____

_____

DAY 9

40 Days of Finding Favor

"And the Lord said unto Moses, Hew thee two tables of stone like unto the first: and I will write upon these tables the words that were in the first tables, which thou brakest."
~Exodus 34:1~

Elul is the time for the miracle of God's mercy in our lives. In Exodus 34:1, God commanded Moses to reascend Mount Sinai to receive the second set of stone tablets. Prior to this event, Moses had descended from the Mount after receiving God's laws for Israel from God Himself, only to find Israel steeped in the sin of idolatry with the golden calf. Moses had then broken the first set of tablets upon which God's laws were written.

The time from Elul 1 to Yom Kippur are days designated with destiny. They mark the 40 days Moses went up the mountain to receive the second set of God's Commandments. In Hebrew, these days of predestined purpose and promise are called *Yemei Ratzon* (Days of Favor). You may ask the question: How are these days on the Biblical calendar separated and consecrated for days of finding favor? It was through this second set of the Law that Israel became reinstated after what their sin as a nation had obliterated.

The second set was a prophetic prefiguring and a foreshadowing of Christ's work at Calvary's cross and the new testament of His blood, which can be seen as the "second" work in God's plan to redeem His own people. In Exodus 34:1, the text goes out of its way to tell us that Moses had broken the tablets. This is a prophetic foreshadowing of how we all "like sheep have gone astray" by breaking God's Law, but then found favor with God through the blood of His son, Jesus Christ. It is an essential element in our Rosh Hashanah experience to understand that the month of Elul is a time of favor and grace.

Upon descending Mount Sinai, when Moses discovered Israel going astray in returning to their idolatrous practices from Egypt, God said to Moses in Exodus 32:10, *"Now therefore let me alone, that my wrath may wax hot against them, and that I may consume them: and I will make of thee a great nation."* Through their sin, the children of Israel had disqualified themselves from destiny by saying, *"These be thy gods, O Israel, which brought thee up out of the land of Egypt"* (Exodus 32:4).

Just as Moses had shattered in pieces the two tablets in his anger against Israel, so have we broken every single part of God's Law and made ourselves unworthy of His great goodness toward us. The Bible tells us that, no matter how hard Moses pleaded with the Almighty, he could not provide an appropriate atonement to re-establish Israel back into the status they had simply received by the merit of their forefathers. Moses' prayer on behalf of Israel was one that pleaded for such favor and grace in the sight of God.

Exodus 33:13
Now therefore, I pray Thee, if I have found grace in Thy sight, shew me now Thy way, that I may know Thee, that I may find grace in Thy sight: and consider that this nation is Thy people.

When Moses prayed for grace, he prayed that God would show him "Thy way." Upon the very moment he had prayed for the grace and the favor to see and know God's Way, Moses experienced an encounter with Jesus Christ as the Eternal Word, the Pre-Existent One. In Exodus 33:19, God promised Moses that He would cause all of His mercy and goodness to pass before him. It was on the basis of God's favor, goodness, and mercy that would enable Moses to see God's glory up on the mountain and receive the "second set." This goodness and mercy revealed unto Moses would be revealed in the form of a Person.

Exodus 33:19

And he said, I will make all my goodness pass before thee, and I will proclaim the name of the Lord before thee; and will be gracious to whom I will be gracious, and will shew mercy on whom I will shew mercy.

Where it says, *"I will proclaim the name of the Lord before thee,"* according to the context in which this part of the verse is written, it should read: "I will proclaim *My Name* before thee." In this perspective, the text literally means that it is the Lord who will proclaim the name of the Lord. This concept corresponds with Psalm 110:1: *"The Lord said unto my Lord, Sit thou at my right hand, until I make thine enemies thy footstool."* Moses had an encounter with the Lord Yeshua, prefiguring that there is no other way to receive the favor and the grace of God, except through Him.

Through this experience, the text teaches that what occurred hundreds of years later on the Mount of Transfiguration also occurred here on Mount Sinai. This is why the evangelists Matthew, Mark and Luke tell us that Moses was present on that mountain. The very words used by Luke are used in Exodus 34:5, *"And the Lord descended in the cloud, and stood with him there, and proclaimed the name of the Lord."*

When Moses came down from the mountain 40 days later, it was Yom Kippur. For ancient Israel, this was the nation's holiest day of the year. Yom Kippur is the day when blood is placed upon the mercy seat, and sins are forgiven and covered, prophetically foreshadowing the work of the cross. We, who were "strangers" and "aliens from the commonwealth of Israel," have been brought "nigh by the blood of Christ" (Ephesians 2:12-13), making us eligible for the 40 Days of Favor, *Yemei Ratzon.* God wants to bestow His favor upon you. In the name of Jesus, as you prepare for Rosh Hashanah, we claim that the Almighty will go before you and prepare the way for your destiny by His favor.

Exodus 33:14-17

And he said, My presence shall go with thee, and I will give thee rest. And he said unto him, If thy presence go not with me, carry us not up hence. For wherein shall it be known here that I and thy people have found grace in thy sight? Is it not in that thou goest with us? So shall we be separated, I and thy people, from all the people that are upon the face of the earth. And the Lord said unto Moses, I will do this thing also that thou hast spoken: for thou hast found grace in my sight, and I know thee by name.

Nehemiah 2:7a

Moreover I said unto the king, If it please the king, let letters be given me.

During these 40 days of finding favor, we claim that the same favor given to Nehemiah through letters granted by the king (representing God's word and authority), so shall you have favor to go forward this year into your destiny by the power of His Word. This Rosh Hashanah, just as Joseph had miraculous favor with Pharaoh, so shall it be given unto you by those who are called to open doors of destiny on your behalf. At this very moment, some of you are in a place where the enemy has set a trap to destroy you, but you shall find divine favor with the King, just as Esther had found favor with the king.

<u>Esther 2:15</u>

Now when the turn of Esther, the daughter of Abihail the uncle of Mordecai, who had taken her for his daughter, was come to go in unto the king, she required nothing but what Hegai the king's chamberlain, the keeper of the women, appointed. And Esther obtained favour in the sight of all them that looked upon her.

Today, we are believing God for you to carry an anointing of such favor, that it may be found in the sight of all who look upon you.

The Supernatural Season for Your Divine Turnaround

Prayer

Lord Jesus, this Rosh Hashanah, we claim these promises as a favor to Your precious blood through the blessing of Your mercy in the "second set." Precious Savior, let the mantle of Your grace and favor, be upon me in the sight of all those who look upon me. I shall receive this request, not based on what I have done, but based only upon who You are. Thank You, dear Jesus. The destiny You have prepared for me is so great and so massive that, as I begin this new year, I know I could never accomplish it by anything I possess, but only by what You have done. I declare that I shall boldly possess all the promises You have purchased for me by Your grace and by Your favor, in the mighty name of Jesus. Amen.

Spiritual Goals
Making Decisions for Destiny

1) Do I struggle with the bondage of self-condemnation?

_____

_____

_____

_____

_____

2) Do I disqualify myself from destiny based on my failures?

_____

_____

_____

_____

_____

Breakthrough for Blessing Guide

Every time the voice of condemnation tries to discourage you out of your destiny, make the decision this year to claim divine favor, just as Israel received such favor through the One whose goodness passed before him.

Immerse yourself on a daily basis in love, forgiveness, mercy, and the goodness of Jesus Christ. Ask Him to reprogram your mind if you have been *guilt*-oriented. Instead of being guilt-oriented, claim that you will be *grace*-oriented.

_____

_____

_____

_____

_____

_____

_____

_____

_____

_____

_____

DAY 10

The Agreement Anointing: The Potency and Power for the Impossible in Your Life

"And all the people gathered themselves together as one man into the street that was before the water gate.... And Ezra the priest brought the law before the congregation both of men and women, and all that could hear with understanding, upon the first day of the seventh month."
~Nehemiah 8:1a, 2~

Have you ever wondered: What is the most damaging deterrent to destiny in a life? Throughout Scripture, the text teaches how the destiny destroyer of strife can deter us away from possessing God's promises far more than any other type of destruction. In Ezra 3:1, we see the result of God's hidden hand miraculously maneuvering history, kings, and world events in order to bring His people back from the dark days of Babylonian captivity. We also see that divine providence had engineered this encounter to occur on Rosh Hashanah.

Ezra 3:6a
From the first day of the seventh month began they to offer burnt offerings unto the Lord.

In Ezra 3:1 and Nehemiah 8:1-2, the text teaches that it was God's predestined plan to move these monumental miracles into motion on Rosh Hashanah. These miracles were orchestrated and coordinated to occur at the "set time" because of the unbreakable bond of unity between the settlers. In both books of Ezra and Nehemiah, the context conveys how the predetermined destiny of God's perfect timing was placed into action when they all came together as "one man."

Ezra 3:1b
"The people gathered themselves together as one man to Jerusalem."

Nehemiah 8:1a
"And all the people gathered themselves together as one man."

The Supernatural Season for Your Divine Turnaround

In the books of Ezra and Nehemiah, we see this "oneness of Spirit," which is one of the most powerful Biblical success secrets left as a legacy for every succeeding generation to uphold. The synonymous circumstance in both texts is the fact that these miracles occurred on Rosh Hashanah. The text also summarizes and prioritizes that those who had returned to their land from captivity had made definite decisions for the new year for a strife-free environment. By applying certain disciplines for destiny, the settlers were already determined to never entertain or tolerate any form of discord.

The continuity in both Ezra and Nehemiah demonstrate that coming together as one man involved *cheshbon hanefesh* (thought and motive assessments), the spiritual accounting in their souls to remain strife-free. "Oneness of Spirit" means: though diversified, they were unified through the absence of all strife. When we choose to vacate a situation brewing with strife and division, we remain on a path that ensures no blocks to the blessing God wants to pour upon us for the new year.

Psalm 133:1 says, *"Behold, how good and how pleasant it is for brethren to dwell together in unity!"* The text goes on to tell us that there is a power-producing property in unity of the Spirit that releases and increases the anointing to its highest potential and purpose in our lives. Continuing on, Psalm 133:2 describes this property as *"the precious ointment upon the head* (the anointing) *that ran down upon the beard, even Aaron's beard: that went down to the skirts of his garments."* Then the Bible says in Psalm 133:3, *"for there the Lord commanded the blessing."* Wherever there is complete and absolute unity, without strife, the Lord will command His blessing.

In 2 Chronicles 5:13, the text teaches how "oneness of Spirit" intensifies and magnifies the power of His presence to its highest, greatest potential upon the earth. The context conveys that the anointing had reached its highest culmination and greatest revelation, which can only be achieved through the absence of disunity.

2 Chronicles 5:13

It came even to pass, as the trumpeters and singers were as one, to make one sound to be heard in praising and thanking the Lord; and when they lifted up their voice with the trumpets and cymbals and instruments of musick, and praised the Lord, saying, For he is good; for his mercy endureth for ever: that then the house was filled with a cloud, even the house of the Lord.

Strife can disqualify us from destiny and can cause catastrophic consequences. Scripture teaches that Moses was denied entrance into the land of promise due to strife and the waters of strife. As the new year approaches, let us make the decision to put away strife every day from our lives. It is my prayer, beloved, that your destiny will supernaturally soar into the highest place of promise by asking God to keep your life free from strife by His grace.

The Supernatural Season for Your Divine Turnaround

Prayer

Lord, I ask that You grant me the grace to not insist on my own way, and to not desire always having the "last word." Instead, may Your "law of kindness" always be on my tongue by Your favor and by Your grace. This year, I command all blockages against my blessings to be removed. Since strife cannot coexist with Your blessing and the anointing, I claim a strife-free life, Lord. Grant me the grace to only bless and pray sincerely for my enemies, no matter what may be said to me or about me. Lord, I ask You to increase the anointing on my life, and may my destiny be a sweet-smelling savor in Your sight. Let my destiny be a place for Your Presence always, filled with the full manifestation of the blessings and the promises You have for me to give You all the glory, in the name of Jesus. Amen.

Spiritual Goals
Making Decisions for Destiny

1) When have I been tempted this week to say something that could have hurt someone or brought a division?

_____

_____

_____

_____

2) What are some Scriptural, Christ-like ways that I can respond when someone accuses me falsely or speaks behind my back?

_____

_____

_____

_____

3) What are some Scripture verses that I can write in my journal and pray over every night to help me respond in a gentle and meek manner whenever I am hurt, crushed or gossiped about by others?

_____

_____

_____

_____

Breakthrough for Blessing Guide

Learn to love the Lord's Prayer. Make a list of secret spiritual challenges that you are asking God for the grace to overcome.

Pray for the person who hurt you the most and speak Scripture verses of blessing over them with sincerity and truth.

Watch God open phenomenal doors of destiny as you apply these tools of blessing and principles for breakthrough into action.

Know that you will be greatly rewarded for making these very difficult decisions for destiny!

_____

_____

_____

_____

_____

_____

_____

_____

The Supernatural Season for Your Divine Turnaround

The Supernatural Season for Your Divine Turnaround

_____

_____

_____

_____

_____

_____

_____

_____

_____

_____

_____

_____

_____

_____

_____

_____

_____

_____

_____

_____

_____

_____

_____

_____

_____

DAY 11

Guarding the Gates

"Set a watch, O Lord, before my mouth;
keep the door of my lips."
~Psalm 141:3~

Your next dimension of destiny during Rosh Hashanah requires a time of preparation, self-examination, and supernatural transformation of character. Attitudes and the way we see the future must also be carefully scrutinized and examined. Rosh Hashanah is a new time, a supernatural season, contingent on introspection and character correction. It is the time where we step into a new destiny so vast that it will require removing the blocks off the blessings and parting with the patterns of the past that have placed our destinies on hold. Stepping into a new destiny requires self-confrontation and personal examination by doing *cheshbon hanephesh* (soul accounting). In actuality this requires that we make an investment in the spiritual assessment of our overall character.

The Supernatural Season for Your Divine Turnaround

Throughout the Bible, the text teaches that the design of destiny is released in our lives through passing tests. A test for your destiny is the examination for the qualification needed to advance to your next level of destiny. God has prepared a plan that will enable us to regain lost time and territory. The month of Elul, the sixth month before Rosh Hashanah, which is the first day of the seventh month, has been designated and consecrated for as days of self-confrontation and interior examination.

The word *Elul* is related to the Aramaic word for "search." This means during Elul we submit ourselves to the search. Jeremiah 29:13 says, *"And you shall seek Me and you shall find Me when you search for Me with all your heart."* During the sixth month we ask God to reveal any personality patterns or secret sins that lie deep in our hearts. Sometimes in the business of life we "shove" and "stuff" our personal pain deep in the innermost parts of our hearts. Elul is the time all secrets come to the surface. One of the ways we are able to come into perfection through character correction is through "guarding the gates."

The Supernatural Season for Your Divine Turnaround

Every Elul just before Rosh Hashanah, one of the passages into the pathway of the "search" is found in Deuteronomy 16:18, which says, *"Judges and officers shalt thou make thee in all thy gates which the Lord thy God giveth thee throughout thy tribes."* In a personal prophetic sense, let us also "appoint judges and officers" over our gates. These gates are the areas where we become most vulnerable to sin. David appointed guards at the gates to prevent sin with his emotions and words. He set up and "appointed guards at the gates" to put a constraint over himself so he would not miss his moment for breakthrough and destiny.

The text that helps us understand how David set guards at the gates of his words and emotions is found in 1 Chronicles 12:1, which states, *"Now these are they that came unto David to Ziglag while he yet kept himself close because of Saul the son of Kish."* The phrase "held himself close" comes from the Hebrew word *atsar*, which means "to hold back." This means that his examination was for exaltation to the next level of destiny.

The text teaches that David "held himself back." This means there were many things David could have done while he was being pursued daily by

Saul. However, David chose *atsar*, "to hold himself back," from what he wanted to do and say in this very unjust, untrue persecution, which stemmed out of pure jealousy. David set "guards at the gates."

Psalm 39:1
I will take heed to my ways that I sin not with my tongue: I will keep my mouth with a bridle while the wicked is before me.

Psalm 141:3
Set a watch, O Lord, before my mouth; keep the door of my lips.

David set guards over his gates. Therefore, let us "appoint the officers and judges" of God's Word over our emotions and mouth. This is the examination for qualification into destiny. We will not take revenge (get even) by repaying evil for evil.

Romans 12:17
Recompense to no man evil for evil.

Matthew 5:44
[Jesus said,] *But I say unto you, Love your enemies,*

bless them that curse you, do good to them that hate you, and pray for them which despitefully use you, and persecute you.

Beloved, you must remember that the officers spoken of in Deuteronomy 16:18 are the rational faculties of your conscience. Scripture says in 1Timothy 3:9, *"Holding the mystery of faith in a pure conscience."* This means that our conscience has been formed by the Commandments and the teachings in the Word.

The Supernatural Season for Your Divine Turnaround

Prayer

Oh, Jesus, son of David, my King and my Lord, I ask you to give me the grace to guard the gates of all my senses in the upcoming year. I ask You to create in me a unique sensitivity to the Holy Spirit when I say something with my mouth or when I think unkind critical thoughts toward others. Transform me before this new year. Grant me the opportunity to set out on a new path, so that I might embark upon the destination for the greatest exultation of destiny in my life. I do not want to block the blessings by my attitude or thought patterns that are not conformed to Your Word. Thank you, Jesus, for the victory and for the best year of my life! Amen.

Spiritual Goals
Making Decisions for Destiny

1) Are there areas in my life that I need to decide upon now to place guards in the gates?

_____
_____
_____
_____

2) Do I have "the last word syndrome complex"? Do I always need to have the last word to prove myself right?

_____
_____
_____
_____

3) Do I spend time daily in prayer with a healthy examination of conscience?

_____
_____
_____
_____

The Supernatural Season for Your Divine Turnaround

Blessing for Breakthrough Guide

Write down an episode or situation of someone who deeply hurt you, disappointed you, or gossiped against you. After reading about guarding the gates, will you respond to them the same way you did before?

Write down some new ways you will avoid the temptation of retaliating, speaking evil, or thinking unkind thoughts about the person who hurt you.

Ask the Lord how you can do good for someone who has done something that hurt you deeply.

Expect a blessing, a breakthrough, and doors of destiny to open wide as you walk in this path faithfully and consistently.

_____

_____

_____

_____

_____

_____

The Supernatural Season for Your Divine Turnaround

DAY 12

The Secret of The Search

*"And ye shall seek Me, and find Me,
when ye shall search for Me with all
your heart."*
~Jeremiah 29:13~

Preparing for the promises of Rosh Hashanah can be summed up in the "secret of the search." This incredible journey begins in the month of Elul. The word *Elul* is similar to the word for "search" in Aramaic. This means God has chosen for this month to be savored with reflection and introspection right before the blessings, breakthroughs, and destiny. The process of removing the bondages off the blessings is called *cheshbon hanephesh*. In Hebrew, the concept of *cheshbon hancphesh* means "accounting of the soul." Engaging in the process of *cheshbon hanephesh* (a personal accounting of the soul) will bring us to a place of inner transformation through self-examination. This is a time where we contour our character traits and emotions to be just like Jesus through His grace.

In a personal prophetic sense, the road to Rosh Hashanah is contingent on the concept of self-scrutiny. One of the greatest examples in the Bible of how *cheshbon hanephesh* is successfully completed can be seen in the life of King David. King David inherited the character trait of self-scrutiny from his forefather Judah. The name Judah is taken from the Hebrew root *moda*, which means "to admit." The secret of the search and its high place of priority is revealed by David in Psalm 26.

Psalm 26:1-2

Judge me, O Lord; for I have walked in mine integrity: I have trusted also in the Lord; therefore I shall not slide. Examine me, O Lord, and prove me; try my reins and my heart.

In Psalm 26:1-2, the text teaches that King David submitted himself to the search. This is the perfect illustration of self-examination through *cheshbon hanephesh*.

The Supernatural Season for Your Divine Turnaround

Looking at the text more closely we see the phrase try my reins. In Hebrew, the phrase "try my reins" refers to the faculties in our hearts that purify the emotions. The word "reins" in Hebrew is *kilyah*, which can also mean "kidneys." The reins are the purifiers of our thoughts just as the kidneys act as purifiers of the blood. This means the process of self-scrutiny begins with using God's Word to detox from us bitterness, envy, strife, or any emotion that can block the blessings in our lives.

The text teaches that this *blamelessness* is our destiny.

Ephesians 1:4
According as he hath chosen us in him before the foundation of the world, that we should be holy and without blame before him in love.

Philippians 2:15
That ye may be blameless and harmless, the sons of God, without rebuke, in the midst of a crooked and perverse nation, among whom ye shine as lights in the world.

To walk blameless before God means that we must have truth within (Psalm 51:6). We must utilize

The Supernatural Season for Your Divine Turnaround

the filtering faculties that lay in our hearts and within our consciences for self-scrutiny so that we too can walk blameless before God.

Hebrews 5:14

But strong meat belongeth to them that are of full age, even those who by reason of use have their senses exercised to discern both good and evil.

1 Timothy 1:5

Now the end of the commandment is charity out of a pure heart, and of a good conscience, and of faith unfeigned.

The Supernatural Season for Your Divine Turnaround

Prayer

My King and My God, I submit myself to the search. I ask You to search my heart and reveal to me if there are any unchecked motives, words, or thoughts that I have allowed in my life. I ask You for the grace of self-scrutiny skills. Help me to stretch into the stature of the fullness of Christ so that I may possess every promise You have ordained this Rosh Hashanah, in the name of Jesus. Amen.

Spiritual Goals
Making Decisions for Destiny

1) Have I been in denial about any motives or behaviors that are not rooted in integrity and the love of God?

_____

_____

_____

_____

2) How will I sharpen my self-scrutiny skills and place all my thoughts, emotions, and actions before Him as part of my daily curriculum?

_____

_____

_____

_____

3) Am I aware of my vulnerabilities and susceptibilities that might make me fall into temptation?

_____

_____

_____

_____

Blessing for Breakthrough Guide

Create a *Decision for Destiny* log. List the Scripture verses that will guide you into blessing and breakthrough for the upcoming year.

_____

_____

_____

_____

_____

_____

_____

_____

_____

_____

_____

_____

_____

_____

_____

_____

The Supernatural Season for Your Divine Turnaround

DAY 13

The Miraculous Manifestation of the Impossible in Your Life

"And the Lord visited Sarah as he had said, and the Lord did unto Sarah as he had spoken. For Sarah conceived, and bare Abraham a son in his old age, at the set time of which God had spoken of him."
~Genesis 21:1-2~

The multiple miracles of Rosh Hashanah begin with the breakthrough of Isaac's birth. After 10 tests and years of tears and trials, Abraham was ready to possess his promise.

Genesis 21:5-6
And Abraham was an hundred years old, when his son Isaac was born unto him. And Sarah said, God hath made me to laugh, so that all that hear will laugh with me.

The Supernatural Season for Your Divine Turnaround

In Hebrew, the name Isaac is *Yitzchak*, which means "laughter." The rabbis teach that the miracle of Isaac's birth took place on Rosh Hashanah. Everywhere throughout the world on the first day of Rosh Hashanah, Genesis 21 is read.

The holy laughter around the birth of Isaac was because it was a miracle of the impossible. God wants you to know that as you prepare to seek Him with all your heart, your soul, your mind, and your strength, He also wants to do the miracle of the impossible in your life. Luke 1:37 says, *"For with God nothing shall be impossible."*

There are two destiny dynamics proven to us in the life of Abraham. During the month of Elul, we have the opportunity to prepare for possession of these promises as we activate them in our lives for the new year.

The first destiny dynamic to possess the impossible in your life is the Supernatural Secret of Wholeheartedness Before God:

The Supernatural Season for Your Divine Turnaround

Genesis 17:1-2

And when Abram was ninety years old and nine, the Lord appeared to Abram, and said unto him, I am the Almighty God; walk before me, and be thou perfect. And I will make my covenant between me and thee, and will multiply thee exceedingly.

God told Abraham that the contingency for this covenant was to walk before Him and be wholehearted, meaning to maintain the quality of *tamimus* (purity of heart, blamelessness, or integrity). As children of the Most High God, we have obtained favor and grace to walk before Him in the destiny of blamelessness. Ephesians 1:4 says that *"ye be found in Him holy and without blame before Him in love."* This means that we must treasure what Jesus did for us on the cross, and never allow our hearts to be tainted with bitterness, untruth, guile, ambition, pride, or anything that is not Christ-like.

The second destiny dynamic to possess the promises of the impossible is Faith:

Genesis 15:6 says, *"And he believed in the Lord; and He counted it to him for righteousness."* During this month of Elul, let us search our hearts for any unbelief that has interrupted our life of faith.

Let us appropriate this faith: *"Who against hope believed in hope, that he might become the father of many nations, according to that which was spoken, So shall thy seed be. And being not weak in faith, he considered not his own body now dead, when he was about an hundred years old, neither yet the deadness of Sarah's womb: He staggered not at the promise of God through unbelief; but was strong in faith, giving glory to God; And being fully persuaded that, what he had promised, he was able also to perform* (Romans 4:18-21).

Please watch these next verses, beloved, so we know that what God has promised Abraham, He has also promised us: *"Now it was not written for his sake alone, that it was imputed to him; But for us also, to whom it shall be imputed, if we believe on him that raised up Jesus our Lord from the dead"* (Romans 4:23-24). Beloved, let us live in faith!

Prayer

Wonderful Savior, I believe You are the God of the impossible. I claim this season of Rosh Hashanah as my season of the Miraculous Manifestation of the Impossible in my life. I claim that everything You did for Abraham—what is written in your Word according to Romans 4:23-24—is also for me. I declare that during this month, in preparing for the promises of Rosh Hashanah, that I will receive the anointing for the impossible in my life. In the name of Jesus, amen!

Spiritual Goals
Making Decisions for Destiny

1) Am I trusting God and confessing His Word concerning the impossible in my life? Explain.

_____

_____

_____

_____

2) Are there areas of unbelief in my life that I need to trust God in greater measure for? Am I in His Word daily?

_____

_____

_____

_____

3) Is my expectation level unmovable because it is grounded in God's Word? Explain.

_____

_____

_____

_____

The Supernatural Season for Your Divine Turnaround

4) Am I trusting God and going before him daily to give me the grace to purify my heart before him and walk before Him perfectly (blamelessly)?

_____

_____

_____

_____

Breakthrough for Blessing Guide

Select Scripture verses about faith that you will confess on a daily basis and pronounce during the new year.

_____

_____

_____

_____

_____

_____

_____

_____

_____

_____

_____

_____

_____

_____

DAY 14

The Supernatural Suddenlies of Rosh Hashanah: Out of the Pit into Your Promise

"Then Pharaoh sent and called Joseph, and they brought him hastily out of the dungeon: and he shaved himself, and changed his raiment, and came in unto Pharaoh."
~Genesis 41:14~

Have you ever asked God, "Why?" or "What did I do, God, that this should happen to me?" Immediately, we begin to make assessments, and try to figure out what went wrong or where we "missed it." Some of us begin to put our memories on "rerun" like a tape. It seems the deeper we dig, and the more we begin to analyze the things that have happened in our lives, the sooner we start to feel that things just do not seem to match up or make sense. The question then arises, "Why do bad things happen to good people?"

Beloved, if anyone ever could have asked those questions, it could have been Joseph. The Bible does not document any details about how Joseph felt when he endured all the trials and afflictions that he encountered. For Joseph, there seemed to be one trial after another in his life. Then finally, after it appears that he is gaining some ground after the traumatizing betrayal of his brethren, he is then falsely accused for something that he blatantly refused to participate in and simply did not do. When we face similar situations in our lives, we cannot help but ask the question, "How could God allow this?" If we look a little more carefully into Joseph's situation, we will understand that all the things he endured were stepping stones to his highest elevation into destiny.

Genesis 39:20

And Joseph's master took him, and put him into the prison, a place where the king's prisoners were bound: and he was there in the prison.

The text indicates to us that there were two prisons. One was the common prison and the other was the king's prison where political prisoners were bound. These prisoners were individuals that served Pharaoh intimately. In the king's prison, Joseph was elevated to being the keeper of the prison and there he could learn everything he needed to know about Pharaoh and his court. And it was on Rosh Hashanah that he would be pulled up out of the pit into his highest purpose as ruler over Egypt. The power of providence orchestrated and coordinated Joseph's promotion into the palace.

Again, this miracle occurred on Rosh Hashanah! It was on this day that Joseph was **pulled up out of the pit into his purpose**. Genesis 41:14 says, *"Then Pharaoh sent and called Joseph, and they brought him hastily out of the dungeon: and he shaved himself, and changed his raiment, and came in unto Pharaoh."* After 13 years of tears, God's decree of destiny was issued for Joseph.

Leviticus 23:24
Speak unto the children of Israel, saying, In the seventh month, in the first day of the month, shall ye have a sabbath, a memorial of blowing of trumpets, an holy convocation.

A "memorial" is known as a *zikaron*. This is why one of the names of Rosh Hashanah is *Yom*

HaZikaron (Day of Remembrance). The day the Almighty ordained that Joseph should come up out of the pit and into the promise was on Rosh Hashanah. This miraculous moment with destiny occurred as a result of *remembrance.*

In Genesis 41:9, the text specifies the use of the words, *"I do remember."* These were the words used by the chief butler of Pharaoh when Pharaoh was seeking a man to interpret his dreams. It was there in the dark dungeon that Joseph accurately interpreted the dreams of the baker and the butler. The text teaches in Genesis 40:14 that Joseph said to the chief butler, *"But think on me when it shall be well with thee, and show kindness, I pray thee, unto me, and make mention of me unto Pharaoh, and bring me out of this house."* It was upon the remembrance of what Joseph had done for the butler in the prison that the butler made mention of him unto Pharaoh.

The text refers to this miracle by using the words "I remember." Genesis 41:9 states, *"Then spake the chief butler unto Pharaoh, saying, I do remember my faults this day."* Throughout the text, the context conveys several symbols of Rosh Hashanah, including the use of the number 7 in a superfluous manner. The number 7 is repeated over 17 times so that we will connect to the concept that the day God remembered Joseph was the first day of the seventh month, which was on Rosh Hashanah.

During this season, after long trials and tests, God wants to shift you out of the pit and into the promises He has ordained for you. God wants you to know that He has seen your suffering and your sorrow. He knows what you have been through in these years of tears. Feeling forgotten can be one of the most painful emotions we can ever experience. The miracle of Rosh Hashanah that was given to Joseph is one of the greatest decrees of destiny in the Bible. As you prepare for the "supernatural suddenlies" of Rosh Hashanah, just as Pharaoh sent and called for Joseph, God is calling you into His perfect promises for this new year. God is going to do "supernatural suddenlies" for you just as He did for Joseph!

Psalm 40:2
He brought me up also out of an horrible pit, out of the miry clay, and set my feet upon a rock, and established my goings.

That supernatural suddenly of being transitioned out of that painful place and into the palace is written in God's Word to give you hope. Your heavenly Father has an expiration date on these trials and tests. He wants you to know He has not forgotten you. This is the season of preparation for the greatest impartation of destiny in your life!

The Supernatural Season for Your Divine Turnaround

Prayer

My dearest King, I offer you my life to be used for Your glory in this new year. I do believe that on Rosh Hashanah You shall remember me. I stand on your word according to Malachi 3:16, that the book of remembrance will be opened "on that day." I believe you will remember me on that day. I claim that on this Rosh Hashanah I will come up out of the pit into my promise for the glory of God! I claim that what You did for Joseph, You will do for me, in the name of Jesus. Amen!

Spiritual Goals
Making Decisions for Destiny

1) Do I feel that I have been lowered into a pit and forgotten by God? If so, explain why.

_____

_____

_____

_____

2) What comparisons in my life do I see with Joseph, Jeremiah, or with any other person that was lowered into a pit?

_____

_____

_____

_____

3) Am I trusting the God who pulled up David, Jeremiah, Joseph, and Daniel out of the pit to pull me out of my situation?

_____

_____

_____

_____

4) Do I realize that what God did for them, God will do again?

_____

_____

_____

_____

The Supernatural Season for Your Divine Turnaround

Blessing for Breakthrough Guide

Make a list of all the things you are believing God to remember this Rosh Hashanah that you believe will launch you into the next phase of your destiny.

_____

_____

_____

_____

_____

_____

_____

_____

_____

_____

_____

_____

_____

_____

_____

_____

DAY 15

The Promise of Rest After Your Test: God Is Faithful to Stop This Storm

"And God remembered Noah, and every living thing."
~Genesis 8:1a~

"And the ark rested in the seventh month, on the seventeenth day of the month, upon the mountains of Ararat."
~Genesis 8:4~

The waters of the flood in the days of Noah can be compared in context to the flood of many trials and tribulations that happen in our lives. As we prepare to enter into the new year, God wants you to know that His almighty plan for you is a plan for good and not for evil (Jeremiah 29:11).

In Genesis 8, as the time of the flood came to an end, the text gives us dates and months for a reason. This is the very first time in the Scriptures after the creation process that the text gives us dates with months.

Scripture includes these unusual appearances of the phrases "the seventh month" (Genesis 8:4) and "God remembered Noah" (Genesis 8:1) as deliberate details so we may know that the beginning of the end of the flood started on Rosh Hashanah, the Day of Remembrance. This is why the Bible goes out of its way to tell us that the ark rested in the seventh month, for the number 7 represents a separated segment of time in Genesis.

The entire eighth chapter of Genesis emphasizes the supernatural secret of time during the Biblical feasts. God wants you to know that no matter how deep your waters are now during this season of the seventh month, you can trust Him that they will come to an end. Genesis 8 and Rosh Hashanah declare God's promise of re-creation after your devastation.

Trials and tempests can be very difficult. The ark represents the Lord as your Shelter in the time of your storm. Though you may be in the midst of the deepest waters of trials and tribulations, God will protect His elect. You are "sheltered in the time of storm."

Psalm 91:1-2

He that dwelleth in the secret place of the most High shall abide under the shadow of the Almighty. I will say of the Lord, He is my refuge and my fortress: my God; in Him will I trust.

Isaiah 4:6

And there shall be a tabernacle for a shadow in the daytime from the heat, and for a place of refuge, and for a covert from storm and from rain.

I believe God is giving you this word today to prepare you for the promise of this new year: *"When thou passeth through the waters, I will be with thee; and through the rivers, they shall not overflow thee: when thou walkest through the fire, thou shalt not be burned; neither shall the flame kindle upon thee"* (Isaiah 43:2).

In a personal prophetic sense of Scripture, Genesis 8:4 concerns itself with the emphasis on the seventh month. The verse says: *"And the ark rested in the seventh day of the month . upon the mountains of Ararat."* The Hebrew word *Ararat* means to "reverse the curse." The emphasis on the symbol of 7 signifies "rest." For example, Genesis 2:2 says, *"On the seventh day God rested."*

Just as the waters covering the earth were turned off, so is God going to stop your storm and give you rest. You may ask, "When is this dark dilemma ever going to end?"

2 Corinthians 4:17 says, *"For our light affliction, which is but for a moment, worketh for us a far more exceeding and eternal weight of glory."* Beloved, your deliverance is coming!

The Supernatural Season for Your Divine Turnaround

Prayer

Dear Jesus, I ask you to help me trust You in the midst of the storm. I know I will get to the other side, just as you told your disciples, "Let us go over to the other side." I know on the other side there is blessing and breakthrough. I claim that during the seventh month that I will "rest in the test" for the glory of God. I thank You that just as the waters turned when You remembered Noah, even so on this Rosh Hashanah, the Day of Remembrance, You will remember me for Your glory! In the name of Jesus, amen!

The Supernatural Season for Your Divine Turnaround

Spiritual Goals
Making Decisions for Destiny

1) Am I well aware of those in the Bible that God rewarded after their days of testing?

_____
_____
_____
_____

2) Do I truly believe that God will reward me after a time of testing?

_____
_____
_____
_____

The Supernatural Season for Your Divine Turnaround

Breakthrough for Blessing Guide

Select an individual in the Bible who went through a time of severe testing. Explain how you can relate to the person who was tested.

Describe what the outcome was after that person was tested, and the visible increase that you can see in that person's life after the trial.

Trust God to bring rest after the test! The Lord God will deliver His promises to you!

_____

_____

_____

_____

_____

_____

_____

_____

_____

_____

The Supernatural Season for Your Divine Turnaround

_____

_____

_____

_____

_____

_____

_____

_____

_____

_____

_____

_____

_____

_____

_____

_____

_____

_____

_____

_____

_____

DAY 16

Deliverance from Secrets Under the Surface

"Search me, O God, and know my heart: try me, and know my thoughts: and see if there be any wicked way in me, and lead me in the way everlasting."
Psalm 139:23-24

The word used for "search" in the Hebrew language, *chaqar* (Strong's Hebrew 2713), means "to examine intimately." In Psalm 139:23-24, King David requested of God to know his heart and to try him. This means that his relationship with the Almighty was built upon self-scrutiny. David welcomed and invited truth in his inward thoughts to be brought before God.

David's request did not mean that God was not fully aware of the origin of every thought. Rather, Psalm 139 was a prayer of praise to God for His omniscience. David wanted to stay hidden in the secret place where there is no deception. His desire was to give God permission to deal with any brokenness that would affect his rational faculties. As we prepare for Rosh Hashanah, we are asking God to deliver us from secret faults that affect our inward discernment skills.

Psalm 19:12

Who can understand his errors? Cleanse thou me from secret faults.

We want a pure heart before God, for no good thing will be withheld from the one who walks uprightly before Him (Psalm 84:11). As we prepare for the new year, we want to give Him permission to search us and to speak His truth into us. Psalm 103:14 guides us into a deeper deliverance process that prepares us for the season of success that the Lord has ordained during this time of Rosh Hashanah.

Psalm 103:13-14

Like as a Father pitieth His children, so the Lord pitieth them that fear Him. For He knoweth our frame; he remembereth that we are dust.

Your Heavenly Father knows everything about you. "He knoweth our frame" is a concept that will help us understand how deep deliverance is available from those secrets under the surface.

The Hebrew word for "frame" is *yetser* (Strong's Hebrew 3336). The *yetser* is the foundation that forms from the origins of thoughts lodged within our minds. When we read the words of King David who said, *"O Lord, Thou hast searched me and known me ... for there is not a word in my tongue, but, lo, O Lord, thou knowest it altogether"* (Psalm 139:1, 4), we see that God understands our weaknesses, vulnerabilities, and entire personality structure.

Deliverance from secrets under the surface refers to deliverance from the hidden pain and hurts in our hearts that have not been dealt with. Pain in our interior self when not processed properly can lead to wrong thoughts, and these thoughts can lead to attitudes. When preparing for the promises of Rosh Hashanah, we want all blocks removed off any blessings God has ordained to give us.

The book of Esther teaches us the supernatural steps of how we possess our miraculous moments with destiny. The Bible says in Esther 2:9a, *"and the maiden pleased him, and she obtained kindness of him; and he speedily gave her her things for purification, with such things as belonged to her."*

"With such things as belonged to her" in a personal prophetic sense of Scripture means there are certain things that God has ordained that belong to you for your destiny. There are blessings, breakthroughs, and miracles you are going to need to accomplish the assignment that God has given to you. Through Christ, you can possess the many things that belong to you that God has ordained for you before the foundation of the world.

The text further teaches that Hegai "speedily gave her her things [necessary] for purification." If we have attitudes or character traits that are not Christ-like, there can be blocks on the "blessings that belong to us." As we prepare for the promises of Rosh Hashanah, like all of those who walked in the highest design of destiny in their lives, we too must submit ourselves to an internal search of our characters. The search will result in self-confrontation that leads to transformation of character.

The Supernatural Season for Your Divine Turnaround

I hear God saying that the fiery furnace of testings that you have gone through will be greatly rewarded. I sense the Spirit of the Lord giving you this word from Psalm 71:20-21, *"Thou which hast shown me great and sore troubles shalt quicken me again, and shalt bring me up again from the depths of the earth. Thou shalt increase my greatness and comfort me on every side."*

The Supernatural Season for Your Divine Turnaround

Prayer

My dear Father, Thank You for loving me, searching me, and knowing me. I ask You to bring up any secrets under the surface and unrooted in truth that have been lodged in my heart. I want this new year to start with a new cycle of power, restoration, and liberation from all levels of brokenness and any denial within my soul. My desire is to be found pleasing in Your sight, Lord, I want You more than anything else, for I know that having a heart with these *kavanot* (intentions, motives) is truly the secret to success this new year. In the name of Jesus, amen!

Spiritual Goals
Making Decisions for Destiny

1) Am I walking with "truth in the inward parts"?

_____
_____
_____
_____

2) Which secrets under the surface am I afraid to show God?

_____
_____
_____
_____

3) Am I aware that God knows everything?

_____
_____
_____
_____

Breakthrough for Blessing Guide

Write a Scripture verse you will stand on that you know reflects the Heavenly Father's deep, continual care and concern for you.

Describe changes in your thinking that need to happen, and how you will continually trust in His grace for breakthrough.

Know that God will deliver you from secrets under the surface, so that you can walk in wholeness into your destiny!

_____

_____

_____

_____

_____

_____

_____

_____

_____

_____

The Supernatural Season for Your Divine Turnaround

The Supernatural Season for Your Divine Turnaround

DAY 17

The Atonement Anointing: Blood Evidence and Yom Kippur

"And they took Joseph's coat, and killed a kid of the goats, and dipped the coat in the blood."
~Genesis 37:31~

A torn up coat covered in blood is presented to frail and trembling hands. The tender, compassionate eyes of a white-haired father are raised in unbelief. Looking at the torn, shredded coat, he recognizes that this belongs to Joseph.

You may have been presented with a torn up coat. The shreds on the coat prophetically parallel your personal pain and devastated dreams. You may feel complete desperation without hope of restoration. You may be going through days of distress, but God has promised your success.

There is a miracle in the message of Joseph's coat. Although something may have been violently removed from you, God has given His guarantee that life will be better than before for you.

The Bible goes out of its way to document the details of the coat being dipped in the blood of the goats. In a personal, prophetic sense of Scripture, the blood of the goats connects with the concept of atonement. Moses, the author of Genesis, is presenting his intent (through the blood of the goats) to teach us how God will redeem the dream.

We see "blood evidence" in Genesis 37:31, which says, "And they took Joseph's coat, and killed a kid of the goats, and dipped the coat in the blood."

The text is articulating specific atonement language that becomes a type and foreshadowing of the blood-bought miracles of Calvary's cross. The Day of Atonement symbolizes the sacrifice of Calvary. It produces "blood evidence" so we may fully comprehend the cross.

In Leviticus 16, the context conveys that the offering for Israel's sin on the Day of Atonement was a goat. The text teaches, *"And he shall take the two goats, and present them before the Lord at the*

The Supernatural Season for Your Divine Turnaround

door of the tabernacle of the congregation. And Aaron shall cast lots upon the two goats; one lot for the Lord, and the other lot for the scapegoat" (Leviticus 16:7-8).

After years of tears, Joseph was arrayed with the fine linen of another coat. Genesis 41:42 tells us that *"Pharaoh took off his ring from his hand, and put it upon Joseph's hand, and arrayed him in vestures of fine linen, and put a gold chain about his neck."*

Both coats prophetically prefigure how the blood will bring a destiny from complete devastation to the highest elevation through the work of atonement. Romans 5:11b shows us that *"we also joy in God through our Lord Jesus Christ by whom we have now received the atonement."*

When the day of Yom Kippur arrives on the Biblical calendar on the tenth day of the seventh month, it becomes in God's sight a reflection of the perfection of Calvary. Because 7 is the symbol of God's oath ("oath" and "seven" have the same spelling in Hebrew), God declares that the Biblical feasts are times of manifestation and impartation through an "oath" of the work of the cross of Calvary.

The Supernatural Season for Your Divine Turnaround

Prayer

Dear Lord, I claim the Atonement Anointing of bringing my devastation into the highest elevation of destiny. I claim that during this seventh month, and every time I see the symbol of 7 in the feasts, I will see the oaths You have given that are contingent on the cross. Lord, I thank You for the blood evidence on the coat of Joseph that gives me Your guarantee that You will redeem the dream in my life. In the name of Jesus, amen!

Spiritual Goals
Making Decisions for Destiny

1) How would I describe the torn up coat of my decimated dreams?

_____

_____

_____

_____

2) How is God transforming my disappointment into a divine plan of reversal?

_____

_____

_____

_____

Breakthrough for Blessing Guide

Look for blood evidence throughout the Bible. Claim that your destiny will be like Joseph's, and that you will rise from the pit into your purpose.

Write a prayer in praise to God for the blood that has already bought your divine turnaround.

Every time you see blood evidence in the Bible, remember that God is transforming your devastation into your divine destiny!

_____

_____

_____

_____

_____

_____

_____

_____

_____

_____

_____

The Supernatural Season for Your Divine Turnaround

_____

_____

_____

_____

_____

_____

_____

_____

_____

_____

_____

_____

_____

_____

_____

_____

_____

_____

_____

_____

_____

_____

_____

DAY 18

The Miraculous Manifestation of the Seventh Month

"These are the feasts of the Lord, even holy convocations, which ye shall proclaim in their seasons."
~Leviticus 23:4~

From the beginning, God separated the "seventh" (e.g., seventh day) to be *kadosh* (holy) unto Him. The text teaches that *"on the seventh day God ended His work which he had made, and he rested on the seventh day"* (Genesis 2:2a). We also see in Genesis 2:3a that *"God blessed the seventh day, and sanctified it."*

The seventh is set apart as the day God brought his creation into the pinnacle of perfection. Hidden in the first seventh day is the "finishing factor." This means that when God ended His work, He brought everything He made to its highest pinnacle of perfection.

In Genesis 2, the concept of the seventh symbolizes two spheres of time. The first six days prophetically parallel the physical world and work. The seventh day conveys the concept of ceasing from one's own work. The text teaches in Genesis 2:3 that on the seventh day God *"rested from all His work"* which He had made.

In a personal, prophetic sense of Scripture, the seventh is a symbol of entering into rest through the finished work of the cross. Hebrews 4:10 tells us, *"For he that is entered into His rest, he also hath ceased from his own works as God did from His."*

This means that the seventh conveys the concept of the finished work of the cross. We see God's architectural design of 7 revealed throughout Leviticus 23. All seven Biblical feasts are sequentially profiled in 7's, signifying that the Biblical feasts are days filled with destiny.

Leviticus 23:3
Six days shall work be done: but the seventh day is the sabbath of rest, an holy convocation; ye shall do no work therein: it is the sabbath of the LORD in all your dwellings.

This means that all Biblical feasts are patterned after the first seventh. We enter into God's realm of rest, blessing, and breakthrough as we shift into appointed times and days of destiny.

The miraculous manifestation of the seventh month is ordained by God for you to reach your highest potential and purpose. These are days that He has designed with destiny, predestined for you at the appointed time.

One of the most miraculous manifestations of the seventh month is the return of your loss through the power of the cross. I believe this powerful promise is yours during these days of the seventh month.

Leviticus 25:9-10

Then shalt thou cause the trumpet of the jubile to sound on the tenth day of the seventh month, in the day of atonement shall ye make the trumpet sound throughout all your land. And ye shall hallow the fiftieth year, and proclaim liberty throughout all the land unto all the inhabitants thereof: it shall be a jubile unto you; and ye shall return every man unto his possession, and ye shall return every man unto his family.

The Supernatural Season for Your Divine Turnaround

These are texts that promise restoration and divine liberation: restoration in the return of taken territory, and liberation in the return of the slaves back into their families.

The text places a contingency upon these promises. They must occur in the seventh month, prophetically pointing to the rest and recovery that occurs through the finished work of the cross.

Most importantly, the text goes out of its way to stipulate that these divine reversals can only take place on the Day of Atonement. The Day of Atonement is the only day of the year when the high priest enters into the Holy of Holies and presents the blood on the mercy seat, thereby attaining a *kaphar*, an atonement, for Israel. This foreshadows Calvary, meaning that the return of our loss comes through the power of the cross.

This new year I believe God is preparing your blood-bought breakthrough. God has given His guarantee that you will recover the loss of your land (promises). The returning of captives to their families symbolizes that through the blood of the cross you will get your life back. Everything the enemy has stolen must be returned. The shofar that sounds on Rosh Hashanah and Yom Kippur (Day of Atonement) brings all things in your life back into divine order.

Prayer

Lord Jesus, I thank You for the return of my loss through the power of the cross. I claim that I will enter into the realm of rest, not depending on my own righteousness, but being completely dependent upon the finished work of Calvary's cross. I stand in awe that I do not have to earn my breakthrough, but it has already been bought by the blood. I claim the blood-bought blessing of the return of my land, which is the possession of promises. I also claim that any part of my life that has been taken captive must be returned so that Your name will be glorified in my life. Amen!

Spiritual Goals
Making Decisions for Destiny

1) Am I trusting in my own righteousness or works to fulfill my destiny? (If you are a perfectionist by nature, be sure to recognize that all your achievements are accomplished only through God's grace.)

_____

_____

_____

_____

2) Am I resting and trusting in God to bring restoration and liberation in my life?

_____

_____

_____

_____

Breakthrough for Blessing Guide

List your prayer requests that you know the Lord wants to release to you for His glory, and believe that the Lord will bring you into possession of these promises!

Rest in the goodness of the Lord, and be ready to receive the return of your loss through the power of the cross!

_____

_____

_____

_____

_____

_____

_____

_____

_____

_____

_____

_____

_____

The Supernatural Season for Your Divine Turnaround

_____

_____

_____

_____

_____

_____

_____

_____

_____

_____

_____

_____

_____

_____

_____

_____

_____

_____

_____

_____

_____

_____

The Supernatural Season for Your Divine Turnaround

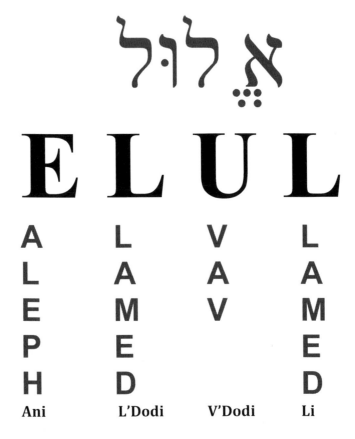

אֱלוּל

E	L	U	L
A	L	V	L
L	A	A	A
E	M	V	M
P	E		E
H	D		D
Ani	L'Dodi	V'Dodi	Li

I am my beloved's, and my beloved is mine.

Song of Songs 6:3

Chesed Publications

What is Chesed?

Chesed means "loving-kindness" in Hebrew. Our publication house is called Chesed Publications because, when you purchase a book, you are helping us do the impossible for people who could never help themselves.

We provide daily feeding programs to orphans and grandmothers, pay for educational fees for children in our orphan homes, conduct medical missions throughout the world, purchase clean water wells, and so much more.

In April 2016, Chesed Publications was founded to financially support Dr. Michelle Corral's vision for acts of chesed to the poor, along with her mission to pass on the wealth of teaching God has entrusted to her to the next generation.

Books Authored by Dr. Michelle Corral

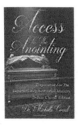  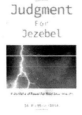 

For a Complete List of CDs and Ministry Resources

Contact:
Breath of the Spirit Prophetic Word Center
P.O. BOX 2676
Orange, CA 92859
Phone # (714) 694-1100

Youtube.com/DrMichelleCorral
Word Network on Mondays
@ 10:30 pm PST

www.breathofthespirit.org
www.drmichellecorral.com
facebook.com/Dr.Corral

22617981R00098

Made in the USA
Columbia, SC
03 August 2018